MITCH MILLER
Community SONG BOOK

A collection for group singing for all occasions including God Bless America

Compiled and Edited by

GUY FREEDMAN

BILL BAILEY

Won't You Please Come Home?

HUGHIE CANNON

Moderato

"Won't you come home, Bill Bai-ley, won't you come home?" She moans the whole day long; "I'll do de cook-ing, dar-ling, I'll pay de rent; I knows I've done you wrong. 'Mem-ber dat rain - y eve dat I drove you out, Wid noth-ing but a fine tooth comb? I knows I'se to blame; well, ain't dat a shame? Bill Bai-ley, won't you please come home." home."

CARELESS LOVE

American Song

3. It's a pity that we met,
   It's a pity that we met,
   Oh, it's a pity that we met,
   For those good times we'll never forget.

4. Cried last night and the night before,
   Cried last night and the night before,
   Oh, I cried last night and the night before,
   Going to cry tonight and I'll cry no more.

5. *(Same as first)*

GIVE MY REGARDS TO BROADWAY

GEORGE M. COHAN

Give my re - gards to old Broad - way And say that I'll be there, e'er long. _____ long. _____

ON TOP OF OLD SMOKY

Southern Mountain Ballad

Tenderly

1. On _ top of Old Smok - y, _____ All _ cov - er'd with snow, _____ I _ lost my true lov - er, _____ Come a - court - in' too slow. _____

2. A-courtin's a pleasure,
   A-flirtin's a grief,
   A false-hearted lover,
   Is worse than a thief.

3. For a thief, he will rob you
   And take what you have,
   But a false-hearted lover
   Will send you to your grave.

4. She'll hug you and kiss you
   And tell you more lies,
   Than the cross-ties on the railroad,
   Or the stars in the skies.

5. On top of Old Smoky,
   All cover'd with snow,
   I lost my true lover,
   Come a-courtin' too slow.

DEAR OLD GIRL

RICHARD HENRY BUCK

THEODORE MORSE

I AM A POOR WAYFARING STRANGER

American Song

TM4302-127

(I'm a) YANKEE DOODLE DANDY

GEORGE M. COHAN

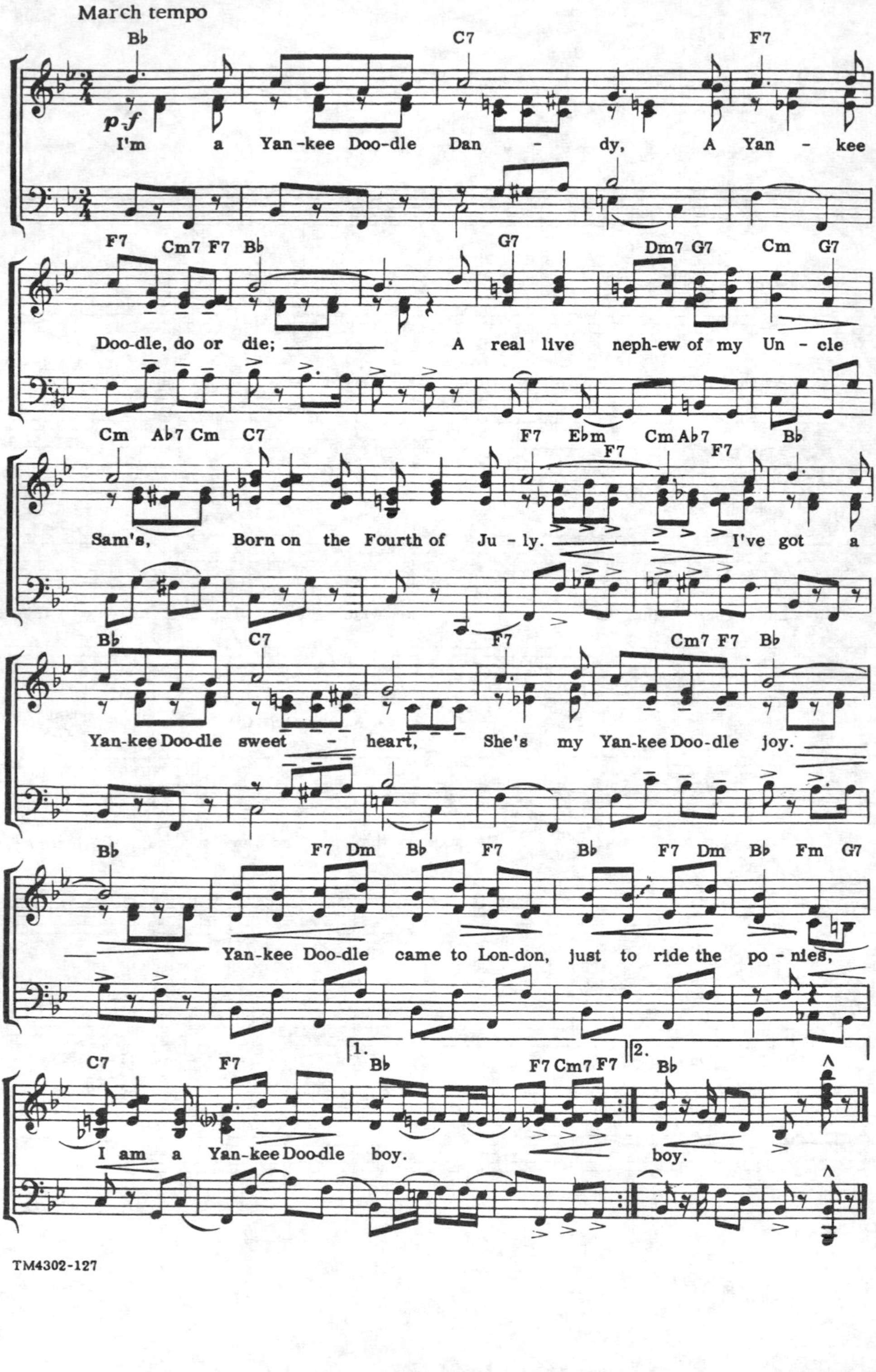

March tempo
Bb C7 F7
pf
I'm a Yan-kee Doo-dle Dan - dy, A Yan - kee
F7 Cm7 F7 Bb G7 Dm7 G7 Cm G7
Doo-dle, do or die; A real live neph-ew of my Un - cle
Cm Ab7 Cm C7 F7 Ebm F7 Cm Ab7 F7 Bb
Sam's, Born on the Fourth of Ju - ly. I've got a
Bb C7 F7 Cm7 F7 Bb
Yan-kee Doo-dle sweet - heart, She's my Yan-kee Doo-dle joy.
Bb F7 Dm Bb F7 Bb F7 Dm Bb Fm G7
Yan-kee Doo-dle came to Lon-don, just to ride the po - nies,
C7 F7 1. Bb F7 Cm7 F7 2. Bb
I am a Yan-kee Doo-dle boy. boy.

IN THE GOOD OLD SUMMERTIME

REN SHIELDS

GEORGE EVANS

In the good old sum - mer - time, _____ In the good old sum - mer - time, _____ Stroll - ing thru the shad - y lanes With your ba - by mine; _____ You hold her hand and she holds yours, And that's a ver - y good sign _____ That she's your toot - sey woot - sey In the good old sum - mer - time. _____

TM4302-127

MARY'S A GRAND OLD NAME

GEORGE M. COHAN

For it is Mar - y, Mar - y, plain as an-y name can be; ___ But with pro-pri - e - ty, so - ci - e - ty will say Ma - rie. But it was Mar - y, Mar - y, long be-fore the fash-ions came; ___ And there is some-thing there that sounds so fair, it's a grand old name! For it is name!

LIST TO THE BELLS

(ROUND)

Anonymous

List to the bells, sil-ver-y bells, Rhym-ing and chim-ing, their mel - o - dy swells, O the beau-ti-ful chim-ing of bells, Bells, bells, chim-ing of bells.

MEET ME IN ST. LOUIS, LOUIS

ANDREW B. STERLING

KERRY MILLS

TM4302-127

MY GAL SAL

PAUL DRESSER

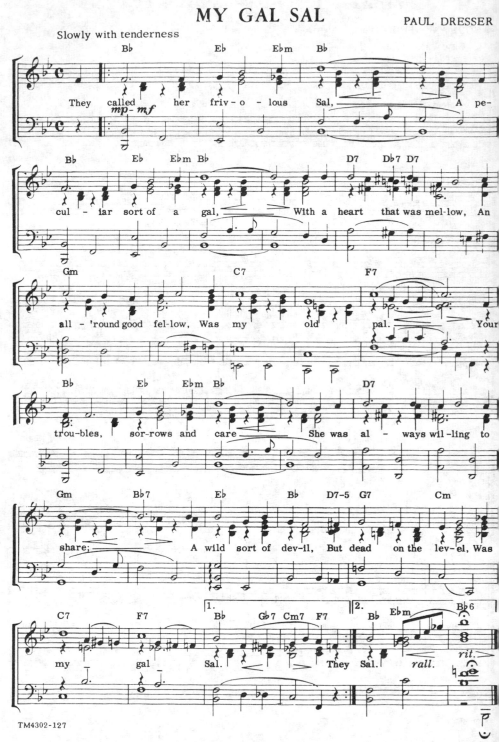

SHE MAY HAVE SEEN BETTER DAYS

JAMES THORNTON

OLD ARK'S A-MOVERIN'

Negro Spiritual

The old ark's a-mov-er-in', a-mov-er-in', a-mov-er-in', The old ark's a-mov-er-in', and I'm goin' home. The I'm goin' home.

old ark she reel, the old ark she rock, Old ark she land-ed on the moun-tain top. Oh, the moun-tain top.

SING TOGETHER

(ROUND)

Sing, sing to-geth-er, Mer-ri-ly, mer-ri-ly sing, Sing, sing to-geth-er, Mer-ri-ly, mer-ri-ly sing, Sing, sing, sing, sing.

SWING LOW, SWEET CHARIOT

Spiritual

D.C. al Fine

SOMETIMES I FEEL LIKE A MOTHERLESS CHILD

Negro Spiritual

LI'L LIZA JANE

American Folk Song

Bright tempo

1. You got a gal and I got none,
2. Liz - a Jane looks good to me,
3. I got a house in Bal - ti - more,
4. Come my love and mar - ry me,

Li'l Liz - a Jane,

Come my love and be my one,
Sweet - est gal I ev - er see,
Pos - ies grow - ing 'round the door,
I will take good care of thee,

Li'l Liz - a Jane.

Oh, E - liz - a! Li'l Liz - a Jane,

Oh, E - liz - a! Li'l Liz - a Jane.

TM4302-127

LONESOME ROAD

American Folk Song

Plaintively

1. Look down, look down that lone-some road,— Hang
   best of friends must part some-time,— Then
2. True love, true love, what have I done,— That
   caused me to walk and talk with you.— Like

Look down, _____ look down that lone-some road, _____

1. F Bbm F
2. F

down _____ your head _____ and cry _____ The
why _____ not you _____ and
you _____ should treat _____ me so? _____ You
I _____ never done _____ be - fore. _____

D.C.
I. _____

LONESOME VALLEY

Spiritual

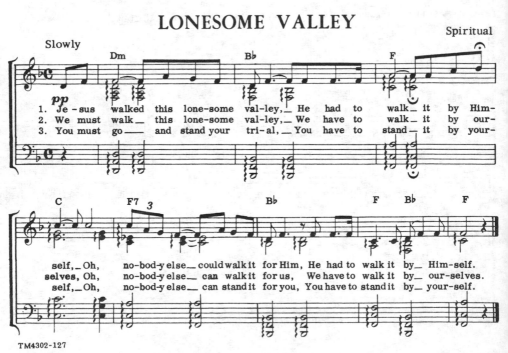

Slowly

1. Je - sus walked this lone-some val-ley,— He had to walk_ it by Him-
2. We must walk_ this lone-some val-ley,— We have to walk_ it by our-
3. You must go_ and stand your tri-al, You have to stand— it by your-

self,_ Oh, no-bod-y else_ could walk it for Him, He had to walk it by_ Him-self.
selves, Oh, no-bod-y else_ can walk it for us, We have to walk it by_ our-selves.
self,_ Oh, no-bod-y else_ can stand it for you, You have to stand it by_ your-self.

DOWN BY THE RIVERSIDE

(Ain't Gonna Study War No More)

Negro Folk Song

Moderato, with fervor

1. Goin' to lay down my bur - den,
2. Goin' to talk with the Prince of Peace,
3. Goin' to meet my King Je - sus,

Down by the riv - er - side, Down by the riv - er - side, Down by the riv - er - side. riv - er - side, to stud-y _____ war no more. _____ I ain't gon-na stud-y war no more; _____ stud-y war no more; _____ stud-y _____ war no more. _____ stud-y _____ war no more. _____

SHORTNIN' BREAD

Traditional

short-'nin', short-'nin', Mam-my's lit -tle {ba-by} {fel -ler} loves short-'nin' bread.

THERE'S A MAN GOIN' 'ROUND TAKIN' NAMES

Negro Spiritual
Harm. by D. M.

There's a man go - in' 'round tak - in' names,

There's a man go - in' 'round tak - in' names,

An' he took my *moth-er's name, An' he leave my heart in

pain, There's a man go - in' 'round tak - in' names.

* father, sister, brother, sweetheart, husband, etc.

TM4302-127

MY LORD, WHAT A MORNING

GOOD-NIGHT

THE LAST ROSE OF SUMMER

THOMAS MOORE   Irish Air

1. 'Tis the last rose of summer, Left blooming a-
2. I'll not leave thee, thou lone one, To pine on the
3. So soon may I follow, When friendships de-

lone; All her lovely companions Are faded and
stem; Since the lovely are sleeping, Go sleep thou with
cay, And from love's shining circle The gems drop a-

gone; No flower of her kindred No rosebud is
them; Thus kindly I scatter Thy leaves o'er the
way; When true hearts lie withered And fond ones have

nigh, To reflect back her blushes, Or give sigh for sigh.
bed, Where thy mates of the garden Lie scentless and dead.
flown, Oh, who would inhabit This bleak world alone.

DRINK TO ME ONLY WITH THINE EYES

BEN JOHNSON

Old English Air

AU CLAIR DE LA LUNE

French Folk Song

Moderately lively

1. With the moon's pale shim - mer, Lit - tle friend Pier - rot,
2. See my lan - tern flick - er, Now the light is out;

Shines thy can-dle's glim - mer, On the fall - en snow.
Now the snow falls thick - er, 'Round and 'round a - bout.

Send a pen, I pray thee, But a word to write,
Gusts go hel -ter, skel -ter, So, the night is old!

One fare-well to say thee Ere I go to - night.
Ope and give me shel - ter Ere I die of cold.

THE BROOM

(Round)

The Netherlands

The broom, the broom, what do you with it, what do you with it? We
sweep with it, we sweep with it, The floor up, the floor up.

O NO, JOHN!

English Folk Song

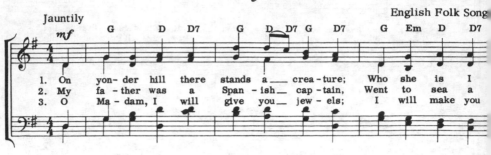

4.
O Madam, since you are so cruel,
And that you do scorn me so,
If I may not be your lover,
Madam, will you let me go?
O no, John! No, John! No, John, No!

5.
Then I will stay with you for ever,
If you will not be unkind.
Madam, I have vow'd to love you;
Would you have me change my mind?
O no, John! No, John! No, John, No!

6.
O hark! I hear the church bells ringing;
Will you come and be my wife?
Or, dear Madam, have you settled
To live single all your life?
O no, John! No, John! No, John, No!

CIELITO LINDO

(Beautiful Heaven)

C. FERNANDEZ

2.
Your bright-eyed glance in the sprightly dance
Lights the shadows, Cielito Lindo;
Here I wait, we must not be late
For the tango, Cielito Lindo.
Ay, ay, ay! *etc.*

TM4302-127

THE GALWAY PIPER

Irish Air

1. Ev-'ry per-son in the na - tion,__ Or of great or hum-ble sta - tion,__ Holds in high-est es - ti - ma - tion Pip-ing__ Tim of__ Gal-way. Loud-ly__ he can play or low; He can move you fast or slow; Touch your hearts or stir your toe, Pip-ing Tim of Gal - way.

2. When the wed-ding bells are ring-ing,__ His the breath to lead the sing-ing,__ Then in jigs the folks go swing-ing, What a __ splen-did__ pip - er. He will blow from eve to morn, Count-ing sleep a thing of scorn; Old is he but not out-worn; Know you such a pip - er?

3. When he walks the high-way peal-ing,__ 'Round his head the birds come wheel-ing;__ Tim has car-ols worth the steal-ing, Pip-ing__ Tim of__ Gal-way. Thrush and lin-net, finch and lark, To each oth-er twit - ter, "Hark!" Soon they sing from light to dark Pip-ings learnt in Gal - way.

THE BIRCH TREE

GRACE BARKER

(Folk Melody used by Tchaikovsky)

Russian Folk Song

Moderately fast

1. See there stands a sil - ver birch - tree, Grow - ing tall and
2. Wake, my dear, and hear me sing - ing; Rise and say a

white in the mead - ow; Liu - lee, liu - lee, in the mead - ow;
pray'r be-fore the i - kon. Liu - lee, liu - lee, liu - lee.

Joy - ous, I will cut the branch- es. I will make three birch-wood
Wear the fin - est coat I made you. Bring your scarf of crim - son and

whis - tles; Steal-ing soft-ly to your win - dow, I will
yel - low; Hur - ry forth and come to meet me. Take my

play you sweet mu - sic; Songs to wake you from slum - ber.
hand and we'll go gai - ly To the birch in the mead - ow.

TM4302-127

THE OLD REFRAIN

FRANCES B. GAINES

(Viennese Lullaby)

Traditional

Smoothly and with feeling

I hear my moth-er sing "Lul-lul-a-bye;" Time has so swift-ly passed, Years seem to fly. Thoughts of my child-hood days come back to me. Moth-er's sweet face in dreams I seem to see. Ah, those are hap-py thoughts, fond mem-'ries bring, Vi-sions of child-hood days, life's joy-ous spring. Sweet then were clo-ver fields,

TM4302-127

| G7 | G7+5 | C | Gm6 A | Dm | G | C7 |

blue skies were clear. Dream-ing, there come to us mem-'ries so dear;

Guitar tacet | F | Bb | Gm *ten.*

And then when eve-ning comes, shad-ows are long; We find a

F | C7 | F

glow-ing fire, we hear a song. On wings of hap-py thoughts

D7 | G7 | F | C7 | F

sweet mem-'ries fly; Once more a moth-er sings "Lul-lul-a-bye."
poco rit.

8va bassa

LOVELY EVENING

Not too slowly   (Round)

Oh! how love-ly is the eve-ning, is the

eve-ning, When the bells are sweet-ly ring-ing,

sweet-ly ring-ing, Ding, dong, ding, dong, ding, dong!

TM4302-127

SANTA LUCIA

Neapolitan Song

Moderately

1. Now 'neath the sil-ver moon O-cean is glow-ing, O'er the calm bil-low Soft winds are blow-ing; Here balm-y breez-es blow; Pure joys in-vite us, And as we gen-tly row, All things de-light us.
2. When o'er thy wa-ters Light winds are play-ing, Thy spell can soothe us All care al-lay-ing; To thee, sweet Na-po-li, What charms are give-en, Where smiles cre-a-tion, Toil blest by heav-en.

REFRAIN

Hark, how the sail-or's cry Joy-ous-ly ech-oes nigh: San-ta Lu-ci-a! San-ta Lu-ci-a! Home of fair Po-e-sy, Realm of pure har-mo-ny, San-ta Lu-ci-a! San-ta Lu-ci-a!

TM4302-127

SKYE BOAT SONG

Sir HAROLD BOULTON, Bart

ANNIE MacLEOD

SWEET MOLLY MALONE
(Cockels and Mussels)

Irish Folk Song

Moderato

1. In Dub-lin's fair cit-y where girls are so pret-ty, I
2. She was a fish-mon-ger, but sure 'twas no won-der, For
3. She died of a fe-ver, and no one could save her, And

first set my eyes on sweet Mol-ly Ma-lone, As she wheel'd her wheel-
so were her fa-ther and moth-er be-fore; And they each wheel'd their
that was the end of sweet Mol-ly Ma-lone; Her__ ghost wheels her

bar-row through streets broad and nar-row
bar-row through streets broad and nar-row } Cry-ing,"Cock-les and Mus-sels, a-
bar-row through streets broad and nar-row

REFRAIN

live, a-live oh! A-live, a-live oh!__ A-live, a-live

oh!"__ Cry-ing, "Cock-les and Mus-sels, a-live, a-live oh!"

COME, FOLLOW
(Round)

Hilton

Allegro

I

Come, fol - low, fol - low, fol - low, fol - low, fol - low, fol - low me.

II

Whith - er shall I fol - low, fol - low, fol - low, Whith - er shall I fol - low, fol - low thee?

III

To the green-wood, to the green - wood, to the green-wood, green - wood tree.

ALOUETTE

French-Canadian Folk Song

Gaily

mf A - lou - et - te, gen-tile A - lou - et - te, A - lou - et - te, Je te plu - me - rai.

D.C.

1. Je te plu-me-rai la tête, Je te plu-me-rai la tête, Et la tête, et la tête.
2. Je te plu-me-rai le bec, Je te plu-me-rai le bec, Et le bec, et le bec.
Et la tête, et la tête.
Oh, —

TALLIS CANON

THOMAS TALLIS

2 - 3 or 4-part

With dignity

Succeeding voices enter here.

Glo - ry to Thee, my God, this night, For all the bless-ings of the light; Keep

me, oh keep me, King of kings, Be - neath Thine own Al - might - y wings.

O, WORSHIP THE KING

SIR ROBERT GRANT

FRANZ JOSEPH HAYDN

1. O, wor-ship the King all glo-rious a-bove, And grate-ful-ly sing, His won-der-ful love; Our Shield and De-fend-er, the An-cient of days, Pa-vil-ioned in splen-dor, and gird-ed with praise.

2. O, tell of His might, and sing of His grace, Whose robe is the light, whose can-o-py space; His char-iots of wrath the deep thun-der clouds form, And dark is His path on the wings of the storm.

3. Thy boun-ti-ful care what tongue can re-cite? It breathes in the air, it shines in the light, It streams from the hills, it de-scends to the plain, And sweet-ly dis-tills in the dew and the rain.

4. Frail chil-dren of dust, and fee-ble as frail, In Thee do we trust, nor find Thee to fail; Thy mer-cies how ten-der! how firm to the end! Our Mak-er, De-fend-er, Re-deem-er and Friend.

TM4302-127

COME YE THANKFUL PEOPLE

HENRY ALFORD   GEORGE J. ELVEY

1. Come, ye thank-ful peo-ple, come, Raise the song of har-vest home:
2. All the world is God's own field, Fruit to His great praise to yield;
3. E-ven so, Lord, quick-ly come, Hold Thy fi-nal har-vest home;

All is safe-ly gath-ered in, Ere the win-ter storms be-gin;
Wheat and tares to-geth-er sown, Un-to joy or sor-row grown:
Gath-er Thou Thy peo-ple in, Free from sor-ow, free from sin;

God, our Mak-er, doth pro-vide For our wants to be sup-plied;
First the blade, and then the ear, Then the full corn shall ap-pear:
There for-ev-er pur-i-fied, In Thy pres-ence to a-bide:

Come to God's own tem-ple, come, Raise the song of har-vest-home.
Lord of har-vest, grant that we Whole-some grain and pure may be.
But the fruit-ful ears to store In His gar-ner ev-er-more.

TM4302-127

THE SPACIOUS FIRMAMENT ON HIGH

(from the "Creation")

JOSEPH ADDISON

FRANZ JOSEPH HAYDN

1. The spa - cious fir - ma - ment on __ high, With __ all __ the __ blue e - the - real _ sky, And span-gled heav'ns, a - shin - ing __ frame, Their great __ O - rig - i - nal __ pro - claim. Th'un - wea - ried sun, from day to day, Does his __ Cre - a - tor's pow'rs dis - play, And pub - lish - es to ev - 'ry

2. Soon as the eve - ning shades pre - vail __ The __ moon __ takes __ up the won - drous tale, And night- ly to the list - 'ning __ earth __ Re - peats __ the __ sto - ry of __ her birth; While all the stars that round her burn, And all __ the plan - ets in __ their turn, Con - firm the ti - dings as they

3. What tho' in sol - emn si - lence __ all __ Move __ round __ the __ dark ter - res - trial __ ball? What tho' no re - al voice nor __ sound __ A - mid __ the __ ra - diant orbs __ be found? In rea - son's ear they all re - joice, And ut - ter forth __ a glo __ rious voice, For - ev - er sing-ing as they

TM4302-127

land   The   work ___   of   an ___   Al - might-y   Hand.
roll,   And   spread ___   the   truth ___   from   pole   to   pole.
shine,   "The   Hand ___   that   made ___   us   is   di - vine."

F. E. WEATHERLY

THE HOLY CITY

STEPHEN ADAMS

Andante moderato

p Last   night   I   lay   a - sleep-ing,   There   came   a   dream so fair: I
   then   me-thought my dream was changed,   The   streets no   long - er rang,

stood   in ___   old   Je - ru - sa-lem,   Be - side   the   tem - ple   there;   I
Hushed were the glad   Ho - san - nas   The   lit - tle   chil-dren sang;   The

heard   the   chil - dren   sing - ing,   And   ev - er   as   they sang,   Me -
sun   grew dark with   mys - ter - y,   The   morn was cold   and chill,   As   the

thought   the   voice   of   an - gels,   From   Heav'n   in   an - swer rang;   Me -
shad - ow   of   a   cross   a-rose   Up - on   a   lone - ly   hill,   As   the

TM4302-127

GLORIA PATRI

English adaptation by
MYRTLE KOON CHERRYMAN

PALESTRINA

THE HEAVENS RESOUND

ANDREAS HOFER

BEETHOVEN

Maestoso

1. The heav'ns re - sound with His prais - es e - ter - nal, In might and
2. The Lord is God! He is King of cre - a - tion; In His right

glo - ry they com - bine To tell His name thro' earth and the
hand He holds them all; His chil - dren, we, in love and de-

o - ceans That man may hear the word di - vine He holds the
vo - tion, Be - fore His might and pow - er fall, O Fa - ther,

suns in the blue vault -ed heav - ens, He plants His foot up - on the
hear! we Thy sons bring our bless-ings, Our pray'r - ful thanks to Thee we

world; The myr - iad stars bow in will -ing sub - jec - tion; The u - ni-
raise; The heav'ns re - sound; break, O earth, in - to glo - ry, To serve a-

TM4302-127

verse His hand un – furl'd, The u – ni – verse His hand un – furl'd.
dore! and sing His praise! To serve! a – dore! and sing His praise!

FROM ILL DO THOU DEFEND ME

JOHANN SEBASTIAN BACH

1. From ill do Thou de – fend me; Re – ceive me, lead me home;
2. New bless-ings dai – ly send me; From Thee all good things come.

Thy love full oft in kind – ness hath milk and hon – ey giv'n; O

heal my mor – tal blind – ness, And fix my heart on Heav'n.

TM4302-127

THE LORD IS MY SHEPHERD

JAMES MONTGOMERY

THOMAS KOSCHAT

1. The Lord is my Shep-herd; no want shall I know.
2. Thro'the val-ley and shad-ow of death tho' I stray,
3. In the midst of af-flic-tion my ta-ble is spread!
4. Let good-ness and mer-cy, my boun-ti-ful God,

Since feed in green pas-tures, safe fold-ed I rest. He lead-eth my
With Thou art my Guard-ian, no e-vil I fear. Thy rod shall de-
bless-ings un-meas-ured my cup run-neth o'er; With per-fume and
Still fol-low my steps till I meet Thee a-bove. I seek, by the

soul where the still wa-ters flow,— Re— stores me when wan-d'ring, re-
fend me, Thy staff be my stay,— No— harm shall be-fall me with my
oil Thou a-noint-est my head; O— what shall I ask of Thy—
path which my fore-fa-thers trod.— Thro' the land of their so-journ, Thy—

deems when op-prest, Re—-stores me when wan-d'ring, re-deems when op-prest.
Com-fort-er near, No— harm shall be-fall me with my Com-fort-er near.
prov-i-dence more? O— what shall I ask of Thy prov-i-dence more?
king-dom of love, Thro'the land of their so-journ, Thy king-dom of love.

THE FIRST NOWELL

Traditional

1. The first Nowell the angel did say Was to certain poor
2. They looked up and saw a star Shining in the
3. This star drew nigh to the North-west, O'er Beth-le-
4. Then entered in those wise-men three, Full rev-'rent-

shep-herds in fields as they lay, In fields where they lay
East beyond them far, And to the earth it
hem it took its rest, And there it did both
ly upon their knee, And of-fered there in

keep-ing their sheep, On a cold win-ter's night that was so deep.
gave great light, And so it con-tin-ued both day and night.
stop and stay Right o-ver the place where Je-sus lay.
His pres-ence, Their gold and myrrh and frank-in-cense.

REFRAIN

ff Now-ell, Now-ell, Now-ell, Now-ell, Born is the King of Is-ra-el.

HARK! THE HERALD ANGELS SING

CHARLES WESLEY

FELIX MENDELSSOHN

1. Hark! the her-ald an-gels sing,_ Glo-ry to the new-born King;
3. Christ, by high-est heav'n a-dored,_ Christ, the ev-er-last-ing Lord;
5. Mild He lays His glo-ry by,___ Born that man no more may die;

Peace on earth and mer-cy mild, God and sin-ners re-con-ciled!
Late in time be-hold Him, come, Off-spring of the vir-gin's womb.
Born to raise the sons of earth, Born to give him sec-ond birth.

2. Joy-ful all ye na-tions rise, Join the tri-umph of the skies;
4. Veil'd in flesh the God-head see; Hail the in-car-nate De-i-ty,_
6. Ris'n with heal-ing in His wings, Light and life to all he brings,

With th'an-gel-ic host pro-claim, Christ is_ born in Beth-le-hem.
Pleas'd as man with man to dwell, Je-sus our Im-man-u-el!
Hail the Sun of Right-eous-ness! Hail, the heav'n-born Prince of Peace.

Hark! the her-ald an-gels sing, Glo-ry_ to the new-born King.

WE THREE KINGS OF ORIENT ARE

J. H. HOPKINS

Tutti: 1. We three Kings of O - ri - ent,
Melchior: 2. Born a King on Beth-le-hem's
Caspar: 3. Frank-in - cense to of - fer have
Balthazar: 4. Myrrh is mine, its bit - ter per -
Tutti: 5. Glo-rious now be - hold Him a-

are; Bear-ing gifts we trav-erse a - far, Field and
plain. Gold I bring to crown Him a - gain, King for -
I; In - cense owns a De - i - ty nigh; Pray'r and
fume, Breathes a life of gath - er - ing gloom; Sor-rowing,
rise, King and God and Sac - - ri - fice, Al - le -

foun - tain, moor and moun - tain Fol - low -ing yon - der star.
ev - er, ceas - ing nev - er, O - ver all to reign.
prais-ing, all men, rais - ing, Wor-ship Him God most High.
sigh -ing, bleed- ing, dy - ing, Seal'd in the stone-cold tomb.
lu - ia, Al - le - lu - ia; Earth to heav'n re - plies.

REFRAIN

Star of won-der, star of night, Star with roy-al beau-ty

bright, West-ward lead-ing, still pro - ceed-ing, Guide us to Thy per-fect light.

TM4302-127

WE WISH YOU A MERRY CHRISTMAS

Happily   Old English Carol

1. We wish you a Mer-ry Christ-mas, We wish you a Mer-ry Christ-mas, We wish you a Mer-ry Christ-mas, And a hap-py New Year! Good ti-dings to you, And all of your kin, Good ti-dings for Christ-mas And a hap-py New Year.

2. Oh, bring us some fig-gy pud-ding, Oh, bring us some fig-gy pud-ding, Oh, bring us some fig-gy pud-ding, And bring it out here!

3. We won't go un-til we got some, We won't go un-til we got some, We won't go un-til we got some, So bring some out here!

CHRISTMAS IS COMING

E. NESBITT

(Three-part Round)

Moderato

Christ-mas is com-ing, the goose is get-ting fat; Please to put a pen-ny in the old man's hat, Please to put a pen-ny in the old man's hat.

IT CAME UPON THE MIDNIGHT CLEAR

EDWIN H. SEARS   RICHARD S. WILLIS

1. It came up-on the mid-night clear, That glo-rious song of old,
2. Still thro' the clo-ven skies they come, With peace-ful wings un-furled;
3. For lo! the days are hast'ning on, By proph-ets seen of old,

From an-gels bend-ing near the earth, To touch their harps of gold:
And still their heav'n-ly mu-sic floats O'er all the wea-ry world:
When with the ev-er-cir-cling years Shall come the time fore-told,

"Peace on the earth, good-will to men From heav'ns all gra-cious King;"
A-bove its sad and low-ly plains They bend on hov-'ring wing,
When the new heav'n and earth shall own The Prince of Peace their King,

The world in sol-emn still-ness lay To hear the an-gels sing.
And ev-er o'er its Ba-bel sounds The bless-ed an-gels sing.
And the whole world send back the song Which now the an-gels sing.

TM4302-127

JINGLE BELLS

JAMES PIERPONT

Lively

1. Dash - ing thro' the snow In a one - horse o - pen sleigh;
2. A day or two a - go I __ thought I'd take a ride,
3. Now the ground is white, _____ Go it while you're young!

O'er the fields we go, Laugh - ing all the way.
Soon Miss Fan - ny Bright was seat - ed by my side. The
Take the girls to - night, and sing this sleigh - ing song. Just

Bells on bob - tail ring, _____ Mak - ing spir - its bright, What
horse was lean and lank, Mis - for - tune seem'd his lot, He
get a bob - tail'd bay, Two - for - ty for his speed, Then

fun it is to ride and sing A sleigh - ing song to - night!
got in - to a drift - ed bank, And we, we got up - sot!
hitch him to an o - pen sleigh And crack! You'll take the lead.

REFRAIN

Jin - gle bells! Jin - gle bells! Jin - gle all the way!

SILENT NIGHT

JOSEPH MOHR

FRANZ GRUBER

1. Si - lent night! Ho - ly night! All is calm, all is bright,
2. Si - lent night! Ho - ly night! Shep - herds quake at the sight!
3. Si - lent night! Ho - ly night! Son of God, love's pure light

Round yon vir - gin moth - er and child! Ho - ly In - fant so ten - der and mild,
Glo - ries stream from Heav - en a - far, Heav'n - ly hosts sing al - le - lu - ia,
Ra - diant beams from Thy ho - ly face, With the dawn of re - deem - ing grace,

Sleep in heav - en - ly peace,— Sleep in heav - en - ly peace.—
Christ, the Sav - ior is born!— Christ, the Sav - ior is born!—
Je - sus, Lord, at Thy birth,— Je - sus, Lord, at Thy birth.—

TM4302-127

TWELVE DAYS OF CHRISTMAS

Traditional
Moderato

Old English

1. The first day of Christ-mas my true love sent to me A par-tridge in a pear tree. 2. The sec-ond day of Christ-mas my true love sent to me Two tur-tle doves and a par-tridge in a pear tree.

*A   B

3. The third day of Christ-mas my true love sent to me   Three French hens,
4. The fourth day of Christ-mas my true love sent to me   Four col-ly birds,
5. The fifth day of Christ-mas my true love sent to me   Five gold rings,

two tur-tle doves and a par-tridge in a pear tree.

6. The sixth day of Christmas my true love sent to me Six geese a-laying,
7. The seventh day of Christmas my true love sent to me Seven swans a-swimming,
8. The eighth day of Christmas my true love sent to me Eight maids a-milking,
9. The ninth day of Christmas my true love sent to me Nine drummers drumming,
10. The tenth day of Christmas my true love sent to me Ten pipers piping,
11. The eleventh day of Christmas my true love sent to me Eleven ladies dancing,
12. The twelfth day of Christmas my true love sent to me Twelve lords a-leaping,

*A-B Repeat this measure as often as necessary, the text in reverse order, always ending with "two turtle doves, etc."

GOD BLESS ALL

(Four part round)
(Sing three times)

1. God bless all 2. Good friends here, A 3. mer-ry, mer-ry Christ-mas and a

*Codetta
(Girls) Mer - ry, mer - ry, mer-ry, mer - ry

4.
Hap - py New Year!
Christ - mas   And a Hap - py New Year!

(Boys) Mer - ry, mer-ry Christ - mas   And a Hap - py New Year!

*After all parts have finished round.

TM4302-127

MARCH OF THE KINGS

(Folk melody used by Bizet)

English text by
FENTON GAYLORD

French Carol from Provence

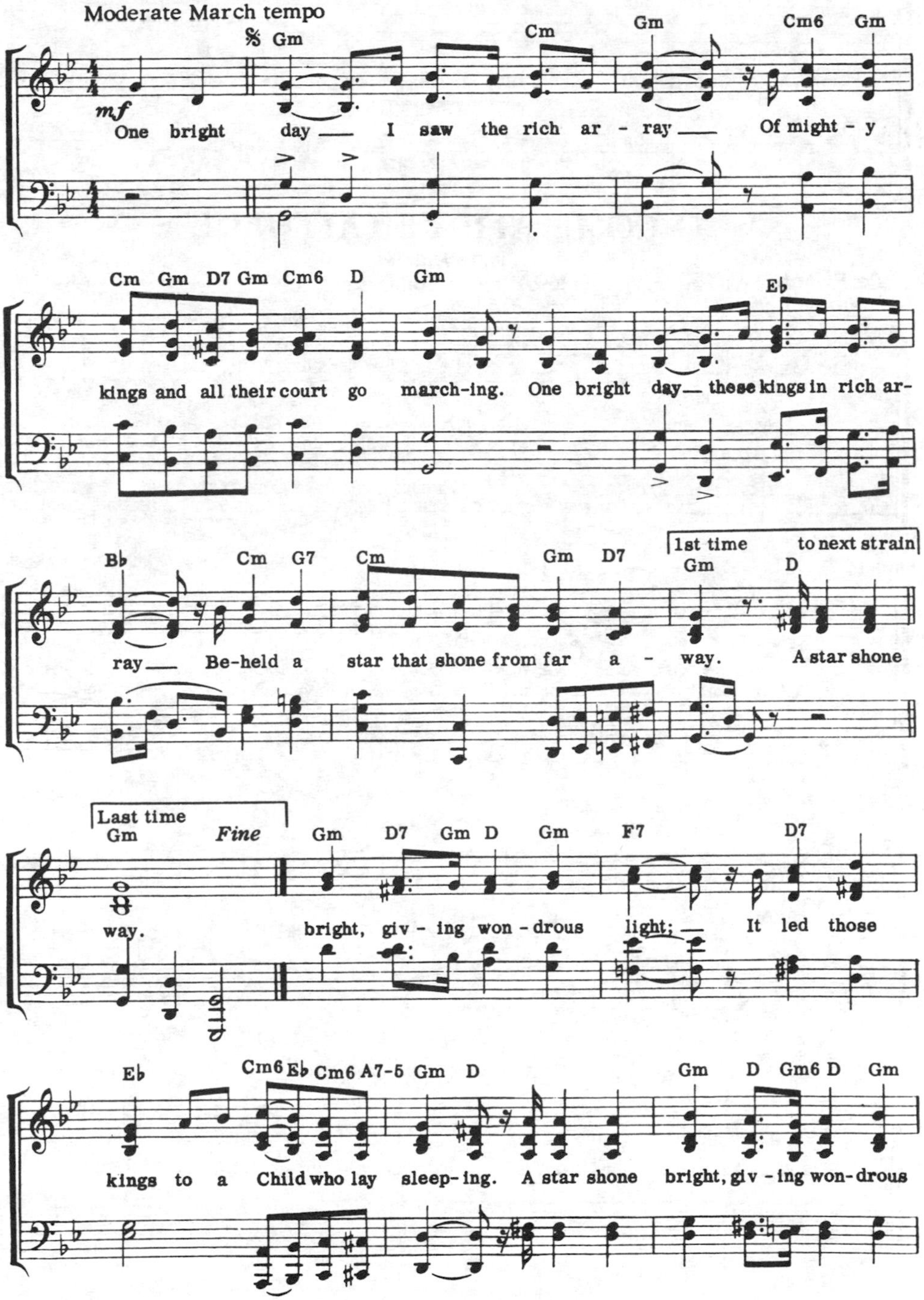

Moderate March tempo
mf
Gm Cm Gm Cm6 Gm
One bright day — I saw the rich ar - ray — Of might - y
Cm Gm D7 Gm Cm6 D Gm Eb
kings and all their court go march-ing. One bright day — these kings in rich ar-
Bb Cm G7 Cm Gm D7
1st time to next strain
Gm D
ray — Be-held a star that shone from far a - way. A star shone
Last time
Gm Fine
Gm D7 Gm D Gm F7 D7
way. bright, giv - ing won - drous light; — It led those
Eb Cm6 Eb Cm6 A7-5 Gm D Gm D Gm6 D Gm
kings to a Child who lay sleep-ing. A star shone bright, giv - ing won-drous

D.S. al Fine

light; They brought Him gifts and knelt down in His sight. One bright

O COME ALL YE FAITHFUL
(Adeste Fideles)
(How Firm A Foundation)

Tr. F. OAKELEY
from the Latin

FRANCIS WADE

1. O come, all ye faith-ful, Joy-ful and tri-um-phant, O
2. Sing, choirs of an-gels, Sing in ex-ul-ta-tion,

come ye, O come ye to Beth-le-hem; Come and be-hold Him
Sing all ye cit-i-zens of heav'n a-bove: Glo-ry to God

Born the King of An-gels:⎰ O come let us a-dore Him, O
In the high-est,⎱

come let us a-dore Him, O come let us a-dore Him,— Christ the Lord.

CANTIQUE DE NOËL

(O Holy Night)

ADOLPHE ADAM

Slowly and majestically

1. O ho - ly night! ___ the stars are bright - ly
2. Led by the light ___ of faith se - rene - ly
3. Tru - ly He taught us to love ___ one an -

shin - ing, It is the night of our dear Sav - iour's
beam - ing, With glow - ing hearts by His cra - dle we
oth - er; His law is love and His gos - pel is

birth; Long lay the
stand; So led by
peace; Chains shall He

TM4302-127

58

world ___ in sin and er - ror pin - ing, Till He ap-
light of a star ___ sweet - ly gleam - ing, Here came the
break, for the slave ___ is our broth - er, And in His

peared and the soul felt its worth. A
wise men from O - ri - ent land. The
name all op - pres - sion shall cease. Sweet

thrill of hope the wea - ry world re - joic - es, For
King of kings lay thus in low - ly man - ger, In
hymns of joy in grate - ful cho - rus raise we, Let

yon - der breaks a new and glo - rious morn; ___
all our tri - als born to be our friend; ___
all with - in us praise His ho - ly name; ___

I HEARD THE BELLS ON CHRISTMAS DAY

HENRY W. LONGFELLOW   J. BAPTISTE CALKIN

Moderato

1. I heard the bells on Christ-mas Day Their
2. I thought how, as the day had come, The
3. And in des-pair I bow'd my head: "There
4. Then pealed the bells more loud and deep: "God
5. Till, ring-ing, sing-ing on its way, The

old fa-mil-iar car-ols play, And wild and sweet the
bel-fries of all Chris-ten-dom Had roll'd a-long th'un-
is no peace on earth," I said, "For hate is strong, and
is not dead, nor doth He sleep; The wrong shall fail, the
world re-volved from night to day, A voice, a chime, a

words re-peat Of peace on earth, good will to men.
bro-ken song Of peace on earth, good will to men.
mocks the song Of peace on earth, good will to men."
right pre-vail, With peace on earth, good will to men."
chant sub-lime, Of peace on earth, good will to men!

SHOO FLY!

Snappy   Old Army Song

m.f

Shoo, fly, don't both-er me! Shoo, fly, don't both-er me!

Shoo, fly, don't both-er me! For I be-long to Com-pany G.

TM4302-127

HOME ON THE RANGE

Cowboy Song

1. Oh, give me a home where the buf-fa-lo roam, Where the deer and the an-te-lope play; _____ Where sel-dom is heard a dis-cour-ag-ing word And the skies are not cloud-y all day.
2. How of-ten at night, when the heav-ens are bright, With the light from the glit-ter-ing stars, _____ Have I stood there a-mazed and _ asked as I gazed If their glo-ry ex-ceeds that of ours. _____

REFRAIN

Home, home on the range, _____ Where the deer and the an-te-lope play, _____ Where sel-dom is heard a dis-cour-ag-ing word And the skies are not cloud-y all day. _____

BIG ROCK CANDY MOUNTAIN

Moderato

Traditional

1. On a sum-mer day in the month of May, A __ bur-ly bum came
2. On a run came a farm-er __ and his son, To the hay fields they were

hik-ing. Down a shad-y lane, thru the sug-ar cane He was
bound-ing. Said the bum to the son, "Why __ don't you come to that

look-ing for his lik-ing. As he roamed a-long he
Big Rock Can-dy Moun-tain?" So the ver-y next day they

sang a song of the land of milk and hon-ey, __ Where a bum can stay for __
hiked a-way, All the mile posts they kept count-ing, __ But they nev-er ar-rived at the

man-y a day and he won't need an-y mon-ey. __ Oh! the
lem-on-ade tide In the Big Rock Can-dy Moun-tain. __

REFRAIN

buzz-in' of the bees in the cig-ar-ette trees, Near the So-da Water foun-tain, At the

lem-on-ade springs Where the blue bird sings, In the Big Rock Can-dy Moun-tain.

BURY ME NOT ON THE LONE PRAIRIE

Plaintively

Cowboy Song

mp

"Oh, bur-y me not _____ on the lone prai - rie,"

These words came low _____ and _ mourn-ful - ly _____

from the pal - lid lips _____ of a youth who lay _____

On his dy - ing bed _____ at the close of day. _____

TM4302-127

RED RIVER VALLEY

Traditional

Slowly

mf

1. From this val - ley they say you are go - ing,— I shall
2. I have prom - ised you dar - ling that nev - er,— Shall the

miss your sweet face and your smile,— Just be-
words from my lips cause you pain,— And my

cause you are wea - ry and tir - ed,— You are
life it shall be yours for - ev - er,— If —

chang - ing your range for a - while.— I've been
you on - ly love me a - gain.— When you

think - ing a long time, my dar - ling,— Of the
think of the val - ley you're leav - ing,— Oh! how

65

TM4302-127

SWEET BETSY FROM PIKE

Flowingly

Folk Song

1. Oh don't you re-mem-ber Sweet Bet-sy from Pike Who cross'd the big moun-tains with her lov-er Ike, With two yoke of cat-tle And a large yel-ler dawg, And a tall Shang-hai roos-ter And one spot-ted hawg? Say-ing

2. On an ev-'ning quite ear-ly They camped on the Platte, Near by the road on a green, shad-y flat; There Bet-sy, quite tir-ed lay down to re-pose While with won-der Ike gazed on his Pike Coun-ty Rose.

REFRAIN

fare-well Pike Coun-ty, Good-bye for a while We'll
come back a - gain Whenve've panned out our pile.

3. They soon reached the desert, where Betsy gave out
   And down in the sand she lay rolling about;
   While Ike very tearful looked on in surprise,
   Saying "Betsy, get up, you'll get sand in your eyes.   –Refrain

4. Then Betsy got up with a great deal of pain,
   And swore she'd go back to Pike County again .
   Then Ike heaved a sigh, while they fondly embraced,
   And she travelled along, with his arm 'round her waist. –Refrain

5. The Shanghai flew off, --the cattle all died,
   The last piece of bacon that morning was fried;
   Ike, he got discouraged, while Betsy got mad
   And the dog wagged his tail, looking awfully sad.   –Refrain

6. Next morning they climbed up a very high hill,
   Looking down in wonder on Old Placerville;
   Ike shouted and said, as he cast his eyes down,
   "Sweet Betsy, my darling, we've got to Hangtown. "   –Refrain

7. Long Ike and sweet Betsy they attended a dance,
   Ike, he wore a pair of his best Sunday pants
   Sweet Betsy was decked out with ribbons and things,
   Said Ike, "You're an angel, but where are your wings?" –Refrain

8. A miner said, "Betsy, will you dance with me?"
   Said Betsy, "I will, if you don't get too free;
   Don't dance me too hard. Do you want to know why?
   Doggone you, I'm chock full of strong Alkali."   –Refrain

9. They married, and afterwards got a divorce,
   And Ike left her everything including his horse;
   Sweet Betsy, quite satisfied, said with a shout,
   "Good-bye, you big lummox, I'm glad you backed out."   –Refrain

Last Refrain: Saying good-bye, dear Isaac,
                Farewell for a while.
                Be sure and come back
                To replenish my pile.

HEAR THE WIND BLOW

TURKEY IN THE STRAW

Traditional

Lively

1. As I was a gwine on down de road With a
2. Went out to milk and I didn't know how,
3. Met a big cat-fish comin' down the stream Says the

tir-ed team and a heav-y load, I cracked my whip and the
Milked the goat in-stead of the cow A mon-key sit-tin' on a
big cat-fish "What does you mean?" Caught the big cat-fish right

lead-er sprung, Says I good-bye to the wag-on tongue.
pile of straw, Wink-in' at his moth-er-in-law.
on the snout, Turned Mis-ter Cat-fish in-side out.

REFRAIN

Tur-key In The Straw (whistle) Tur-key In The Straw

(whistle) Roll 'em, twist 'em up a high tuck-a-haw, And

TM4302-127

hit up a tune called "Tur - key In The Straw."

THE GAL I LEFT BEHIND ME

Traditional
Cowboy Song

A bit lively

1. I struck the trail in sev-en-ty-nine The herd strung out be-
2. If I ev-er get off the trail And the In - dians they don't

hind me As I jogged a - long my mind ran back For the gal I left be-
find me I'll make my way straight back a - gain To the gal I left be-

REFRAIN

hind me.} That sweet lit-tle gal that true lit-tle gal, The gal I left be-
hind me.}

hind me, That sweet lit-tle gal, that true lit-tle gal, The gal I left be-hind me.

3. The wind did blow, the rain did flow,
The hail did fall and blind me;
I thought of that gal, that sweet little gal
That gal I left behind me.
Refrain:

4. She wrote ahead to the place I said
I was always glad to find it.
She says " I am sure when you get through
Right back here you will find me."
Refrain:

5. When we sold out I took the train
I knew where I could find her;
When I got back we had a snack
And that was no gol-darned liar.
Refrain:

TM4302-127

TRAMP! TRAMP! TRAMP!

GEORGE F. ROOT

March tempo

1. In the pris - on cell I sit, Think - ing,
2. In the bat - tle front we stood When their
3. So, with - in the pris - on cell, We are

Moth - er dear, of you, And our bright and hap - py home so far a -
fierc - est charge was made, And they swept us off, a hun - dred men or
wait - ing for the day That shall come to o - pen wide the i - ron

way; And the tears they fill my eyes Spite of all that I can do, Though I
more; But be - fore we reached their lines They were beat-en back, dis-mayed, And we
door; And the hol - low eye grows bright, And the poor heart al-most gay, As we

REFRAIN

try to cheer my com-rades and be gay.
heard the cry of vic-t'ry o'er and o'er. {Tramp! tramp! tramp! the boys are march - ing
think of see-ing home and friends once more.} marching on, O

Cheer up, com-rades, they will come, _____ And be - neath the star-ry flag We shall
cheer up, com - rades, they will come,

breathe the air a-gain Of the free-land in our own be-lov-ed home.

THE PEAT-BOG SOLDIERS

German Prisoner Song

Resolutely

1. Far and wide as the eye can wan-der, Heath and bog are
2. Up and down the guards are pac-ing, No one, no one
3. But for us there is no com-plain-ing, Win-ter will in

ev-'ry-where. Not a bird sings out to cheer us, Oaks are stand-ing
can go through; Flight would mean a sure death fac-ing, Guns and barbed wire
time be past. One day we shall cry, re-joic-ing: Home-land, dear, you're

gaunt and bare. 1.&2. We are the peat-bog sol-diers, We're
greet our view. *mf*
mine at last. 3. Then will the peat-bog sol-diers

march-ing with our spades to the bog. We bog.
March no more with their spades to the bog. Then bog.

TM4302-127

THE STAR-SPANGLED BANNER

FRANCIS SCOTT KEY

JOHN STAFFORD SMITH

AMERICA
(My Country 'Tis of Thee)

SAMUEL FRANCIS SMITH

HENRY CAREY

1. My coun-try 'tis of thee, Sweet land of lib-er-ty,
2. My na-tive coun-try, thee, Land of the no-ble free,
3. Let mu-sic swell the breeze, And ring thru all the trees
4. Our fa-thers' God, to Thee, Au-thor of lib-er-ty,

Of thee I sing; Land where my fa-thers died, Land of the
Thy name I love: I love thy rocks and rills, Thy woods and
Sweet free-dom's song; Let mor-tal tongues a-wake; Let all that
To Thee we sing; Long may our land be bright With free-dom's

Pil-grim's pride, From ev-'ry moun-tain-side Let free-dom ring.
tem-pled hills; My heart with rap-ture thrills Like that a-bove.
breathe par-take; Let rocks their si-lence break, The sound pro-long.
ho-ly light; Pro-tect us by Thy might, Great God our King.

TM4302-127

BATTLE HYMN OF THE REPUBLIC

JULIA WARD HOWE

1. Mine __ eyes have seen the glo - ry of the com - ing of the Lord; He is tram-pling out the vin - tage where the grapes of wrath are stored; He hath loosed the fate - ful light - ning of His ter - ri - ble swift sword: His truth is march - ing on.

2. I have seen Him in the watch - fires of a hun - dred cir - cling camps; They have build - ed Him an al - tar in the eve - ning dews and damps; I can read His right-eous sen - tence by the dim and flar - ing lamps: His day is march - ing on.

3. I have read a fi - ery gos - pel writ in bur-nished rows of steel: "As ye deal with My con - tem - ners, So with you My grace shall deal; "Let the He - ro born of wom - an crush the ser - pent with His heel, Since God is march - ing on.

4. He has sound - ed forth the trum - pet that shall nev - er call re-treat; He is sift - ing out the hearts of men be fore His judg - ment seat. Oh, be swift, my soul, to an - swer Him! be ju - bi - lant, my feet! Our God is march - ing on.

5. In the beau - ty of the lil - ies Christ was born a - cross the sea, With a glo - ry in His bos - om that trans - fig - ures you and me; As He died to make men ho - ly let us die to make men free, While God is march - ing on.

REFRAIN

Glo - ry, glo - ry, hal - le - lu - jah! Glo - ry, glo - ry, hal - le - lu - jah!

Glo - ry, glo - ry, hal - le - lu - jah! His truth is march-ing on.

THE BRITISH GRENADIERS

16th Century

March tempo

f 1. Some talk of Al - ex - an - der, and some of Her-cu - les, Of
2. When - e'er we are com - mand - ed to storm the Pal-is - ades, Our

Hec - tor and Ly - san - der, and such great names as these; But of
lead - ers march with fus - es, and we with hand gre - nades; We

all the world's brave he - roes there's none that can com - pare, With a
throw them from the gla - cis, a - bout the en-e-mies' ears, With a

tow, row, row, row, row, row, To the Brit - ish Gren-a - diers.
tow, row, row, row, row, row, The Brit - ish Gren-a - diers.

GOD BLESS AMERICA

Arranged by Wm. C. Schoenfeld

IRVING BERLIN

TM4302-127

AMERICA, THE BEAUTIFUL

KATHERINE LEE BATES

SAMUEL A. WARD

1. O beau-ti-ful for spa-cious skies, For am-ber waves of grain, ____ For
2. O beau-ti-ful for pil-grim feet, Whose stern, im-pas-sioned stress ____ A
3. O beau-ti-ful for he-roes proved In lib-er-at-ing strife, ____ Who
4. O beau-ti-ful for pa-triot dream That sees be-yond the years, ____ Thine

pur-ple moun-tain maj-es-ties A-bove the fruit-ed plain! ____ A-
thor-ough-fare for free-dom beat A-cross the wil-der-ness! ____ A-
more than self their coun-try loved, And mer-cy more than life! ____ A-
al-a-bas-ter cit-ies gleam, Un-dimmed by hu-man tears! ____ A-

mer-i-ca! A-mer-i-ca! God shed His grace on thee, ____ And
mer-i-ca! A-mer-i-ca! God mend thine ev-'ry flaw, ____ Con-
mer-i-ca! A-mer-i-ca! May God thy gold re-fine, ____ Till
mer-i-ca! A-mer-i-ca! God shed His grace on thee, ____ And

crown thy good with broth-er-hood From sea to shin-ing sea. ____
firm thy soul in self-con-trol, Thy lib-er-ty in law. ____
all suc-cess be no-ble-ness, And ev-'ry gain di-vine. ____
crown thy good with broth-er-hood From sea to shin-ing sea. ____

THE MINSTREL BOY

THOMAS MOORE

Irish Melody

With vigor

1. The min-strel boy to the war is gone, In the ranks of death you'll find him; His fa-ther's sword he hath gird-ed on, And his wild harp slung be-hind him. "Land of song!" said the war-rior bard, "Tho' all the world be-trays thee, One faith-ful harp shall praise thee." sword at least thy rights shall guard, One faith-ful harp shall praise thee."

2. The min-strel fell but the foe-man's chain Could not bring that proud soul un-der; The harp he lov'd ne'er spoke a-gain, For he tore its chords a-sun-der, And said, "No chain shall sul-ly thee, Thou soul of love and brav-'ry! Thy songs were made for the pure and free, They shall nev-er sound in sla-v'ry."

WHEN JOHNNY COMES MARCHING HOME

Words and Music by
LOUIS LAMBERT

1. When John - ny comes march - ing home a - gain, Hur - rah!__ Hur-
2. The old__ church bell will peal with joy, Hur - rah!__ Hur-
3. Get read - y for the ju - bi - lee, Hur - rah!__ Hur-

rah!__ We'll give him a heart - y wel - come then, Hur - rah!__ Hur-
rah!__ To wel - come home our dar - ling boy, Hur - rah!__ Hur-
rah!__ We'll give__ the he - roes three times three, Hur - rah!__ Hur-

rah!__ The__ men will cheer, the boys will shout, The la - dies they__ will
rah!__ The vil - lage lads__ and las - sies gay With ros - es they__ will
rah!__ The lau - rel wreath is read - y now To place up - on__ his

all turn out, And we'll all feel gay when John - ny comes march - ing home!__
strew the way, And we'll all feel gay when John - ny comes march - ing home!__
loy - al brow, And we'll all feel gay when John - ny comes march - ing home!__

TM4302-127

YOU'RE A GRAND OLD FLAG

GEORGE M. COHAN

March tempo

You're a grand old flag, you're a high fly - ing flag; And for - ev - er, in peace, may you wave;_____ You're the em - blem of the land I love, The home of the free and the brave._____ Ev -'ry heart beats true, un - der Red, White and Blue; Where there's nev - er a boast or brag;_____ But, should auld ac-quaint -ance be for-got, Keep your eye on the grand old flag. You're a flag._____

TM4302-127

GOD OF OUR FATHERS

DANIEL C. ROBERTS

GEORGE W. WARREN

1. God of our fa - thers, whose al - might - y
2. Thy love di - vine hath led us in the
3. From war's a - larms, from dead - ly pes - ti -
4. Re - fresh Thy peo - ple on their toil - some

hand, Leads forth in beau - ty all the star - ry band;
past, In this free land by Thee our lot is cast;
lence, Be Thy strong arm our ev - er sure de - fence;
way, Lead us from night to nev - er end - ing day;

Of shin - ing worlds in splen - dor thro' the skies,
Be Thou our Rul - er, Guard - ian, Guide and Stay,
Thy true re - li - gion in our hearts in - crease,
Fill all our lives with love and grace di - vine,

Our grate - ful songs be - fore Thy throne a - rise.
Thy word our law, Thy paths our cho - sen way.
Thy boun - teous good - ness nour - ish us in peace.
And glo - ry, laud and praise be ev - er Thine. A - men.

WALTZING MATILDA

Australian Bush Song

1. Once a jol - ly swag - man sat be - side the bil - la - bong,
2. Down came a jum-buck to drink be - side the bil - la - bong,

Un - der the shade of a cou - li-bah tree, And he
Up jumped the swag - man and seized him with glee. , And he

sang as he sat and wait - ed by the bil - la - bong,
sang as he talked to the jum-buck in his tuck - er - bag,

"You'll come a-waltz - ing, Ma - til - da with me."

Waltz-ing Ma - til - da, waltz - ing Ma - til - da,

3. Down came the stockman, riding on his thoroughbred
   Down came the troopers, one, two, three.
   "Where's the jolly jumbuck you've got in your tuckerbag?
   You'll come a-waltzing, Matilda, with me."

REFRAIN
Waltzing Matilda, waltzing Matilda,
"You'll come a-waltzing, Matilda with me"
"Where's the jolly jumbuck you've got in your tuckerbag?
You'll come a-waltzing, Matilda, with me."

4. Up jumped the swagman and plunged into the billabong,
   "You'll never catch me alive," cried he,
   And his ghost may be heard as you ride beside the billabong,
   "You'll come a-waltzing, Matilda, with me."

REFRAIN
Waltzing Matilda, waltzing Matilda,
"You'll come a-waltzing, Matilda, with me."
And his ghost may be heard as you ride beside the billabong,
"You'll come a-waltzing, Matilda, with me."

Note: Swagman - a hobo
Billabong - a water hole in a dried up river bed
Waltzing Matilda - the bundle on a stick carried by a swagman
Jumbuck - a small lamb
Tuckerbag - knapsack

TM4302 127

WHEN IRISH EYES ARE SMILING

CHAUNCEY OLCOTT
and GEO. GRAFF Jr.

ERNEST R. BALL

When I-rish eyes are smil-ing, Sure it's like a morn in Spring. In the lilt of I-rish laugh-ter You can hear the an-gels sing! When I-rish hearts are hap-py, All the world seems bright and gay, And when I-rish eyes are smil-ing, Sure they steal your heart a-way. When way.

MEMORIES

GUSTAVE KAHN

EGBERT VAN ALSTYNE

BY THE LIGHT OF THE SILVERY MOON

ED MADDEN
GUS EDWARDS

By the light _____ of the sil-ver-y moon, _____ I want to spoon, _____ To my hon-ey I'll croon love's tune, Hon-ey moon _____ keep a-shin-ing in June, _____ Your sil-v'ry beams will bring love dreams We'll be cud - dling soon, _____ By the sil-ver-y moon. _____ By the

TWO HEARTS IN 3/4 TIME

W. REISCH, A. ROBINSON
and JOE YOUNG

ROBERT STOLZ

TM4302-127

MOTHER MACHREE

RIDA JOHNSON YOUNG

CHAUNCEY OLCOTT
& ERNEST R. BALL

toil worn for me, Oh, God bless you and keep you, Moth - er Ma - chree!

PUT ON YOUR OLD GREY BONNET

STANLEY MURPHY   PERCY WENRICH

Put on your old grey bon-net with the blue rib - bon on it, While I

hitch old Dob-bin to the shay, _____ And through the fields of

clo - ver, We'll drive up to Do - ver on our gold - en

wed - ding day. _____ Put on your   day.

I'M LOOKING OVER A FOUR LEAF CLOVER

MORT DIXON

HARRY WOODS

TM4301 +97

MOONLIGHT BAY

EDWARD MADDEN

PERCY WENRICH

TM4302-127

I'M FOREVER BLOWING BUBBLES

JAAN KENBROVIN and
JOHN WILLIAM KELLETTE

JUST A COTTAGE SMALL

(By A Waterfall)

B.G.DE SYLVA

JAMES F. HANLEY

Lyrics:

Just a cottage small by a wa-ter-fall, At the clos-ing of the day; With some-one to wait by a gar-den gate Who will charm your trou-bles a - way, Be it hum-ble and all tum-ble down, If there's love to wel-come you, Just a cot-tage small by a wa-ter-fall, Is a place where dreams come [1.] true! Just a place where dreams come [2.] true!

LOUISIANA HAYRIDE

HOWARD DIETZ and
ARTHUR SCHWARTZ

© 1932 WARNER BROS. INC.
Copyright Renewed
All Rights Reserved

FINE AND DANDY

PAUL JAMES

KAY SWIFT

TM4302-127

DANCING IN THE DARK

HOWARD DIETZ   ARTHUR SCHWARTZ

Slowly, with expression

Danc-ing in the dark Till the tune ends, We're danc-ing in the dark And it soon ends; We're waltz-ing in the won-der of why we're here Time hur-ries by, we're here and gone. Look-ing for the light Of a new love to bright-en up the night,

GIVE ME YOUR TIRED, YOUR POOR

Words from the Poem "The New Colossus" by
EMMA LAZARUS

Music by
IRVING BERLIN

Arranged by Wm. C. Schoenfeld

SOMETIMES I'M HAPPY

IRVING CAESAR

VINCENT YOUMANS

TM4302-127

Lyrics (top staff system):
That's how I am, so what can I do?___ I'm hap-py
when I'm with you.___ you.

SWEET GEORGIA BROWN

BEN BERNIE, MACCO PINKARD
and KENNETH CASEY

Moderato

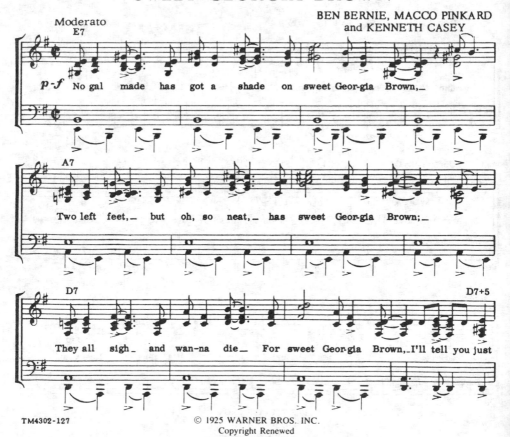

p-f No gal made has got a shade on sweet Geor-gia Brown,___

Two left feet,___ but oh, so neat,___ has sweet Geor-gia Brown;___

They all sigh___ and wan-na die___ For sweet Geor-gia Brown, I'll tell you just

TM4302-127

TM4302-127

ROSE-MARIE

OTTO HARBACH and
OSCAR HAMMERSTEIN, 2nd
Moderato

RUDOLF FRIML

Oh, Rose-Ma-rie, I love you! I'm al-ways dream-ing of you. No mat-ter what I do, I can't for-get you; Some-times I wish that I had nev-er met you! And yet if I should lose you T'would mean my ver-y life to me; Of all the queens that ev-er lived I'd choose you To rule me, my Rose-Ma-rie.

TM4302-127

HALLELUJAH

LEO ROBIN and
CLIFFORD GREY

VINCENT YOUMANS

L'AMOUR-TOUJOURS-L'AMOUR

C. C. CUSHING

RUDOLF FRIML

TIP-TOE THRU' THE TULIPS WITH ME

AL DUBIN

JOE BURKE

French Words: EDITH PIAF

MACK DAVID

LA VIE EN ROSE

LOUIGUY

Slowly, with expression

mp - mf

Hold me close and hold me fast, The mag-ic spell you cast, This is La vie en rose. When you kiss me heav-en sighs, And tho' I close my

TM4302-127

CHARLESTON

CECIL MACK
and JIMMY JOHNSON

MEMORY LANE

B. G. DE SYLVA

LARRY SPIER
and CON CONRAD

TM4302-127

LAUGH! CLOWN! LAUGH!

LEWIS and YOUNG

TED FIORITO

PLAY GYPSIES - DANCE GYPSIES

HARRY B. SMITH

EMMERICH KALMAN

TM4302-127

WITH A SONG IN MY HEART

LORENZ HART

RICHARD RODGERS

Slowly, with rhythm

BLUES IN THE NIGHT

JOHNNY MERCER

HAROLD ARLEN

LULLABY OF BROADWAY

AL DUBIN

HARRY WARREN

Allegro moderato

Come on a-long and lis-ten to ___ the Lul-la-by of Broad-way.

{ The hip-hoo ray and bal-ly-hoo, ___
The hi-dee-hi and boop-a-doo, ___ } the Lul-la-by of Broad-way. ___

{ The rum-ble of a sub-way train, ___
The band be-gins to go to town, ___

The rat-tle of the tax-is,
And ev-'ry one goes cra-zy,

The daf-fy-dils who en-ter-tain ___
You rock-a-bye your ba-by 'round

at An-ge-lo's and Max-ie's. When a Broad-way ba-by says "Good Night;"
'til ev-'ry thing gets ha-zy. "Hush-a-bye, I'll buy you this and that," }

WHEN DAY IS DONE

B. G. DE SYLVA

Dr. ROBERT KATCHER

When day is done and shad-ows fall, I dream of you; When day is done I think of all the joys we knew. That yearn-ing re-turn-ing to hold you in my arms, Won't go, love, I know love, with-out you night has lost its charms! When day is done and grass is wet with twi-light's dew, My lone-ly heart is sink-ing with the sun. Al-

TM4302-127

THE BIRTH OF THE BLUES

B. G. DE SYLVA
and LEW BROWN

RAY HENDERSON

TM4302-127

SOMETHING TO REMEMBER YOU BY

HOWARD DIETZ ARTHUR SCHWARTZ

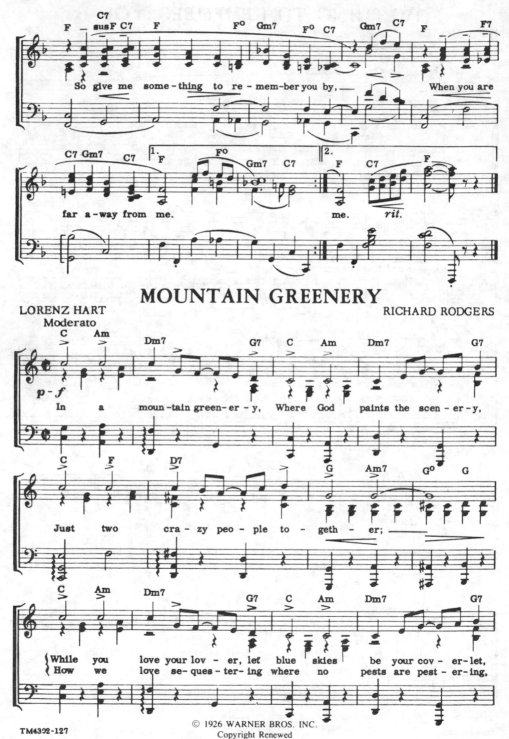

MOUNTAIN GREENERY

LORENZ HART
Moderato

RICHARD RODGERS

So give me some-thing to re-mem-ber you by, When you are far a-way from me. me. *rit.*

In a moun-tain green-er-y, Where God paints the scen-er-y, Just two cra-zy peo-ple to-geth-er;

While you love your lov-er, let blue skies be your cov-er-let,
How we love se-ques-ter-ing where no pests are pest-er-ing,

MY HEART STOOD STILL

LORENZ HART

RICHARD RODGERS

I'M JUST WILD ABOUT HARRY

NOBLE SISSLE and
EUBIE BLAKE

TM4302-127